Ethiopia Boy

CHRIS BECKETT was born in London, but spent an important part of his childhood in Ethiopia, before going on to take a degree in modern languages at Oxford. His poems have been widely published in magazines, and he won first prize in the *Poetry London* competition in 2001 and second prize in the *Chroma* writing competition in 2006. His first collection, *The Dog Who Thinks He's a Fish* (Smith/Doorstop Books, 2004), was described by Moniza Alvi as 'a rare delight'. He has translated poems by the young Ethiopian writer Bewketu Seyoum (*Modern Poetry in Translation*, 2008 and 2012; and *In Search of Fat*, Flipped Eye, 2012) and by the great French Martinican poet, Aimé Césaire.

CHRIS BECKETT

Ethiopia Boy

Oxford*Poets*

CARCANET

First published in Great Britain in 2013 by
Carcanet Press Limited
Alliance House
Cross Street
Manchester M2 7AQ

www.carcanet.co.uk

A CIP catalogue record for this book is available from the British Library
ISBN 978 1 90618 809 2

The publisher acknowledges financial assistance from Arts Council England

Typeset by XL Publishing Services, Tiverton
Printed and bound in England by SRP Ltd, Exeter

Contents

Preface

I grew up in 1960s Addis Ababa, capital of Haile Selassie's glamorous barefoot empire, home of black-maned lions and the African Union, of old priests decked out like butterflies and blazing young singers of Ethio-jazz such as Tilahoun Gessesse and Mahmoud Ahmed.

I wrote my first poem about Ethiopia when I was thirteen, about a python. Many more poems followed but never quite satisfied, as if there was something underneath which my normal language and style could not dig out. Only when I started reading as much Ethiopian poetry as I could find, and after I had a go at translating some Amharic poems myself with the help of a friend, did the real voice of my boyhood come stuttering back to the surface and start to write its own sort of poems.

Ethiopia has more than seventy ethnic groups and languages, so as many poetic traditions. Unfortunately, I am not an expert in any of them. I can only imitate the poems which I have read or heard, and liked, encouraging them to lead me in my own writing. A lot of this poetry is oral or sung. It is only recorded when an enthusiastic researcher like Fekade Azeze or Alula Pankhurst goes into the field to gather verses about a terrible famine, for example, or painful jigger fleas or corrupt politicians. It is an urgent poetry of protest and complaint, as well as praise, sometimes even in the voice of the object of protest, like the famine or the flea, so a sort of ironic boast. And since it is spoken, it delights in the sounds of words and in the physical presence of the people it addresses.

Chris Beckett
2013

Acknowledgements

My thanks to the editors of the following publications in which some of these poems (or versions of them) first appeared: *Ambit, Modern Poetry in Translation, Poetry London, Seam, Smiths Knoll, The Best British Poetry 2011* (Salt), *The Shuffle Anthology 2010/2011* and *Wasafiri*. 'About the fish in Lake Langano' was commended in the Troubadour International Poetry Prize 2008.

Many thanks also to Fekade Azeze for permission to use lines from his book *Unheard Voices: Drought, Famine and God in Ethiopian Oral Poetry* (Addis Ababa University Press, 1998) in my collage poem 'To the man with a guzzler wife'. Also to Bewketu Seyoum and Alemu Tebeje for the chance to learn about Ethiopian poetry direct from two contemporary Ethiopian poets; and to Zerihun Tassew for telling me the story of 'Goat, Donkey and Dog', as well as for his help in finding the house where I lived as a boy in Addis Ababa and through it, what had happened to Abebe.

I am very grateful to Moniza Alvi and Pascale Petit for their advice and encouragement over the years; also to Michael Laskey, David and Helen Constantine, Daljit Nagra, Fred D'Aguiar, John Haynes, Jane Duran, Robert Seatter and the Thursday Group, Jo Roach, Meryl Pugh, Anne Ryland, Valerie Josephs; and Isao Miura for allowing me to use one of his beautiful paintings for the cover of this book.

As long as I, your slim son, am there for you,
why should your home be destroyed?

Mekonnen Galaacha

Abebe, the cook's son

Abebe, from a distant afternoon
Abebe, from an afternoon where everybody naps
even the donkeys propped against trees
    on their little hoofs
Abebe, tall as a eucalyptus tree
Abebe, black all over when he pisses on a eucalyptus tree
who jaunties down dirt tracks to the honey shop
    buys two drippy honeycombs in a box
Abebe, the cool boy in drainpipe jeans and sky-blue sneakers
Abebe, the busy crossing where girls stop to chat
who clicks his fingers to the funky Ibex Band
    as we saunter back up track
Abebe, calling *come here!* to the dog called Come Here
Abebe, trotting round the dog-yard like a horse
who saddles up the smoky horses and takes me prairie-galloping
who makes a dash at mud-caves where hyenas sleep
who shows me how to cook kwalima beef and ginger sausages
    and a chickpea fish for Lent
Abebe, gobbling up the afternoon like a kwalima
Abebe, grinning like a chickpea fish
    while everybody naps

kwalima: a spicy dried sausage made with minced beef and ginger, as well as plenty
   of pepper, cardamom and turmeric

Mount Entoto

Brow of a giant, tufty, full of birds
Dad cuts the engine, calling

chocks away!

so our car swoops down the giant's back
with gasp of tyres

just then a raggy boy appears
flings out his gabi like a bustard's wings

racing down the roadside on small springy feet
on the 't' of take-off

now a fierce astonishing idea flies in the open window

am I leading the wrong life?

all it would take is to open this door
all I must do is to jump out into the wind, shouting

ayzohhhh!!!

but when I turn the handle, with Dad yelling over his shoulder
and our car still plunging like a stone

the boy and his life leap in

gabi: a thick shawl worn over normal clothes for warmth

Bastard saffron

Egg yolk, petrol, honey on coarse bread...

you rebel son of stuffy parents!
piss-brother to a woolly cloth for hermits
who sticks so fast to the long rough threads
not running even when you're boiled

ohoo! you make the boy look at a robe and wonder

   could I be simply colour?

one night he dreams he'll wake up not a boy
     not white or black
but bastard yellow, blind, an attribute...

he is a rich light flooding the bedroom
he is the raffish sweet sound of your name

now he feels bold enough to hug another shape
     and change it! define it!
what will he do with this, who will he love?

adults are like insects, mistaking you for pollen
but you are what the boy sees, how he remembers the future

Praise-shout for Asfaw, the best cook in Africa!

Lips-on-fire! is his spicy lamb
tummy-in-heaven! is his mango jam

awo! he is Mister Cook
our Mister Happiness Cook

his face is rounder than stew-pots
but his fingers run fast as billy goats

his t'ibs cut crisp as a shoe-shine
his fenugreek water, araa! cooler than limes

when he's shredding a fitfit, he whistles
when it's fasting and hushhush, he whispers

dogs howl for his gristly bones
sheep sidle up with muzzling and moans

how can I praise the man who feeds me?
he is my father because he feeds me!

I stand at the iron gates and shout:
Asfaw is the secret I will never let out!

do you know Asfaw, the husband of Almaz?
negus of kitchens and sons?

he cooks all day to feed his families
he is a hundred wooden spoons!

t'ibs: fried meat
fitfit: injera (moist unleavened bread) mixed with spicy stew
hushhush (*shifinfin* in Amharic): stew hidden under a layer of injera, to be ordered
   under one's breath during one of the many religious fasts!
negus: king

Wot?

What's for dinner? Dad calls
flooring bulgy briefcase…
we holler all we're worth
Wot's for dinner, Dad!
his forehead puzzles up
that's what I'd like to know!
by now we're giggling so hard
we nearly wet our pants
three shrieky wriggle-sacks
he scoops to covered basket
tears off ant-hill hat
look! spongy pancake splashed
with knuckle-squirts of stew
and staring eggs, long stick-
tooth shreds of goat, gooey
angel peas and half-bean kikwot

Dad prissies at our fists
tearing food apart
looks on scandal-browed
out, forks! out, schooly Englishness!
we trill, loading our strips
of injera with bombs of
senafich and slither-chicken
drop them on our tongues
three, two, one…..blast-off!!!
then wave our gluey hands
straight up like gum-trees
Asfaw marching in
with bowls and towels, sprays us

in a froth of tut–tuts, scruba–
dubs all reeky colours back to pink
…bar little nubs of black
tucked under our nails
like shrapnel
in the chattery corpse
of our freckle–potato fingers

wot: wot and injera is the Ethiopian national dish, eaten with the fingers. Wot is a
    hot spicy stew made with chicken, beef, eggs, tripe. Strips of injera are used to
    scoop up the wot
kikwot: half-bean stew
senafich: mustard

Motorcar!

the one who roars at gates and donkeys
the one with more doors than a house
the one with two rich tones of skin colour and a flashy
    v-shaped tail
the one who takes neat heads to school
    who takes sorrow to the airport
the one with strange songs bubbling out of his windows
    as he dusts off to market
the one who holds his warm nose out of the mud
    who stuffs a feast of yams in his back pocket
the one we tap and brother as he shoulders along our street
the one who gets a splashy sponge and rub-down
    every morning by his own boy
the one we own with our shiny eyes
the one called *Zephyr*, waxy and proud!

Lion buses

'giving transport service for the city of Addis Ababa from 6.15 a.m. to 9 p.m.'

Nothing-like-a-lion bus!
you who honk and stagger down Progress
    through Cooperation Avenue
you who lick us with diesel, swaying this way and that
with our shopping and hot flesh

where is your pride, lion bus?
where is the lioness to do your hunting of kudu and goat
    while you snooze under a tree?

we don't believe that lions can be buses!
we don't believe that painting *Anbessa* on a bus
    in big gold letters changes you
you slow slug of metal
you cramper of knees and buttocks

yes, there are cars that run like the wolf
there are small trucks as patient as donkeys
but then there are buses, buses…

anbessa: lion (Amharic)

Goat, Donkey and Dog

in the style of Kebede Mikael

Once upon a time, little friend
Goat, Donkey and Dog
took a taxi to the Monday market,
now how should they divide the fare?
with many *ba*s and *haw*s and *bark*s
they finally agreed that
each of them would pay a third,
but Goat searched every fold of skin
and couldn't find a single birr
so he butted at the door and ran away,
then Donkey shook a smallish note
from the wallet of his right ear
and offered it politely clamped
in his long yellow teeth,
while Dog turned paw to palm
and handed over a twenty
crisp as any Monday morning
and waited on the kerb for change.

But the driver was that kind of man
whom God tests by giving him a car
and once behind the wheel
he loses sight of his humanity…
his eyes become narrow and greedy
because he believes that
no one else has such a dashing taxi!
no one else can go as fast as him!
he forgets to say to himself:

Yefat, you have the speed of lizards,
but you cannot make milk like a goat
you cannot cart firewood like a donkey
or guard the house like a dog...
Yefat, you are still just a man
with two legs for walking into church
and two knees for praying!

So all the taxi driver did was laugh
and spit and speed away...
and that is why, little friend,
Goat runs off whenever a car appears,
why Donkey always stands so stiff
and righteous in the middle of the road.
It is also why Dog, poor cheated Dog!
always barks at cars and chases them
and tries to bite their tyres.

Kebede Mikael (1914–1998) was an eccentric and much-loved poet and playwright
who translated *Romeo and Juliet* and *Faust* into Amharic. His poems are often
amusing parables, with titles like *Adamna burrew* ('Adam and his ox') and
Anbessana t'ota ('Lion and Monkey'), in which man and animals complain to God
about their lot and receive his impatient replies.
birr: Ethiopian currency

Horse song

imitation of an ox lament from the Kafa highlands

O, my horse, let me sing!
O, my stormy horse, who neighed
   like a wind in the big rains
   like a drill at the new airport, let me sing!
my horse, who galloped out of rusty gates
whose tail was still in the stable while his head swept
   past the church of Yeka Mikael
O, my horse, let me sing!
O, my speedy horse, who overtook buses of every make
   lorded it over mules and pissed on dung-beetles
your mane was a flag
your legs were marathon runners
you were not for the gharry trot-trot or carty sticks to market
you were not even for the lucky boy to enjoy riding
you were for the pride of being a horse
O, my horse, let me sing!
O, my fidgety horse, who liked to ripple the skin
   up/down your body, let me sing!
you who threw flies off your carpet
who threw dust-writing up in the air, telling other horses
   where you'd gone
O, my horse, where have you gone?
O, my brotherly horse, who took me out of the back seat
   out of the stuffy windows
who rode you after I went away?
who saw the world from your back, felt your blood beating
   under his knees?
O, my horse, let me sing!
O, my sleek horse, what are these shabby bone-bundles
   clopping down Yeka Road?

Wondwossen, the prayer child

after Nega Mezlekia

When you are born as the result of fierce and persistent prayers

when you are born from prayers to all known saints
and from a fortune spent by your mother visiting a holy man
who has just returned from Madagascar and is said to have
the most up-to-date knowledge of the dead and the unborn

when you are born from the gift of a sheep and five kilos
of clarified butter in a tin and a box of expensive oudh

when you are born despite the spells of your father's brothers
to stop another boy inheriting the family's farmland
despite the fact that nobody in the family is a farmer

when you are born and straight away dressed in little frocks
and spend your first four years on earth as a girl called Kutu

when your fourth birthday is marked by the most lavish party
to which four hundred guests are invited, including neighbours
and relations, local bigwigs and their wives, plus all the good
and bad spirits who preside over the town

when your fourth birthday party is also attended by twenty-two
street dogs, seven stray cats and five famished eagles

when your mother brings you out in boy's clothes, with your hair
cut short like a boy, and announces that you are a boy

when everyone is overjoyed except for the evil spirits of
body-snatchers who have no more power

then you know that your speaking soul
   and your thinking soul
   and your soul that is capable of being saved
   and the earth and wind and fire and water
that together make up the seven elements of your being

have been brought into the world because they were all desperately
   wanted by your mother
who will always want you, even when she is dead
   and you are dead

and because of the fierceness of her wanting
you will always want yourself too

Nega Mezlekia's wonderful memoir of his childhood in Jijiga, eastern Ethiopia, is
called *Notes from the Hyena's Belly* (Penguin Books, 2001). Wondwossen was
Mezlekia's best friend and the book is dedicated to him.
oudh: the dark fragrant resin produced in south-east Asia by the agar tree when it
becomes infected with a parasitic mould. It is highly valued for use in perfumes
and incense

What about the scabs on Tamrat's knee?

Are they not juicy like the lips of a cow?
proud as the Battle of Adwa?

up there is the path where a bouda jumped on Tamrat's foot
and knocked him into the dirt

just fifty cents to study this important knee!
my skin-book of adventures!

but quick, the edges are starting to lift like wood-curls
the puss is beginning to freeze

this is the best moment, when the bubbles almost pop out of their
   own heads with squidginess

and if anybody talks to you of wonders
if anyone says

*there is nothing more beautiful in the world than the procession of the Ark
   at Axum!*

if anyone boasts the knuckliest punch in the village
or a blinding skill with numbers

you can answer

well, what about the scabs on Tamrat's knee?

Battle of Adwa: Emperor Menelik II's victory over the Italians in 1896
bouda: evil spirit
the Ark: Menelik I, son of King Solomon and the Queen of Sheba, is said to have
   rescued the Ark from Jerusalem, where it was under attack.

Lemon for love

Today Mahmoud Ahmed is singing again
wailing out of Abebe's radio

lemon for love! lemon for love!
lemon you are so sweet

his voice is long and stringy as a branch
it throws the lemon down at his girlfriend's feet

lemon for love! lemon you are so tasty!
if she picks it up, it means she will marry him

now the chorus is shouting *hohohohoho!*
clapping all its hands, stamping its fifty feet

now Abebe's fingers are jumping and clicking
shoulders shaking! knees popping!

because the girl in the song is beautiful as Makda Queen of Sheba
and yes! she has bent to pick up the lemon

Mahmoud Ahmed, you must never stop singing
your voice can make anything happen

it twists round my brain like the roots of a tree
it opens a fresh leaf in my heart

Mahmoud Ahmed, if I sit here by Abebe's window
will you throw my lemon for me?

Mahmoud Ahmed has been a big star of Ethiopian jazz and big band music from
the 1960s to the present day. He won a BBC World Music Award in 2007. You
can hear him singing *Lomiwen teqebelech* ('She accepted the lemon') on the
Ethiopiques 3 CD from Buda Musique.

Spotted hyenas

In our ears
whooping and tearing

> *write them down!*
> *write them down!*

in the bins at midnight
on the red-moon track

> *write them down!*
> *write them down!*

bones keep them busy
but paper makes them mad

> *write them down!*
> *write them down!*

Berhanu, the nightwatchman

Berhanu who comes tap-tap
past my window

whose walking lulls me sleepy
with his steps so light and comfort

he puts his left shoe down
a toe-weight harder than the right

all other sounds run off
say nothing when Berhanu here

speckled mouse-birds rest their tails
skinks and leaf-ghosts freeze

even the wind is hiding
nervous gates forget to clank

what power he has over the dark spaces
    by the garage
and the jumpy walls!

eyuu! a man who gives peace
to a house he never enters

who vanishes every morning
into my head

An afternoon in the dry season

Zarraaaaf! neighed the horse
with magnificent snorts and shivers

I will gallop to the end of fields
I will frighten the earth to dust
with you, warrior-boy, boasting your kills!

is that you speaking, Abebe?
you joking, in *Horse*?

I have lost your voice
is it a boy who has run off to fetch flour
but he will return soon?
a song I cannot hear, until I open the door?

or are you one of the quiet ones
who speak mostly with their eyes?

your eyes, Abebe! their whites shine
like angels on the wall of a church
like an icon by a Master of the Dark Eyelids
from the sixteenth century

all this horse and hills!
this noisy greeting of the eyes!

zarraaf: the opening formula for warrior boasts, meaning 'plunder' or 'loot'

Abel, the breakfast boy

Mister! you look joyful today
    I smell honey
  on your scrambled eggs, is it
fine to English with you while you eat?

I am Abel, one-leg breathy
    son of Tsegay
  who always jump up quick
to *get-moving!* me out of our crampy tin-tac

listen to my heartfelt story
    when coffee lorry's
  sleepy driver chew
his fat cheek, singing Gigi Shibabew

no stop for wake-up breakfast
    no brake and stop fast
  when I rush in road for sockball
and he knock my leg off like a skittle

mangle-bony better dead!
    the yap-yaps said
  this country needing walk-work
does a camel pay his hay with milky talk?

hoy! Abel's heart was one-leg too
    wearing a shoe
  of *useless boy!* but I am Eng-
lish student now, all Dessie table-footie king

and sometimes I ask tip-top two-legs
    for a plate of eggs
  and honey in the Palace Café
but I eat it upright, sir! not sit-sit like a comfy

Dessie: 'my joy' in Amharic; capital of Wollo province

Dawit at the School of Tomorrow

Battling one giant maths practice-test of multiple-choice
questions to yard it with a bottle of breaktime Fanta,
yanking Gugsa's T-shirt over his rass so he flies off a giggly
and Ato Tassew pats his arm for the truck crash, palm-
shoulders them to Lady's office:

Let's overview your future, boys!

knock-knock! hushy cave of pens and timetables…
Lady whispers, *Heartful sorry for your dad, Dawit*
sniff-sniff… then on to Grade 8 National Exams,
top two per cent win shiny scholarships to the School
of Tomorrow:

but if you fail, you never get past Today!

shy Dawit, orphaned, cowed, but must arise like cream,
bye-bye, Yesterday! no favours for his smash-up dad
or his gentle coughed-out mam, just Aunty Wubit now
two hard-work sisters and a hut, but Tomorrow's burning
with excitement colours:

I can smell the red-hot teachers, Mam!

soon Dawit brisks off home with Gugsa, lugging
satchel-sling of books, mining holey pockets for
one birr he does not have, shadow-buys a red banana
smiling from the stall on Debre Zeyit Road, peels it
pure imagination, shouting:

where will this Dawit be in twenty years???

Dawit: Ethiopian version of David
rass: head
Ato: mister

Addis and Abebe

My name is New, always New.
Even when I'm old, I'll be New.

My friend is Flowering. I wish it was me.
I want to be Flowering when I'm old.

Ibsa's dog

Dog without a name, still too new for names

Ibsa wraps you round his neck
holds your legs lightly just above the paw
so your muzzle rests on his right cheek
and your fur is the softness of trust

Ibsa looks out over the hills
he has painted his face white and brown, like you
he has filled his mouth with milk
to squirt into your mouth

but first he must pick a name for you
will it be
    Ibsa's shadow?
    Ibsa's ears?

in his mind, he whistles for your name to come to him

Earth's greeting to feet

Axee! I greet you, feet of the Afar and the Agaw

feet that cut salt-cakes out of my Great Depression
scribble up gullies and chutes

feet soft as bush-hares with fleshy ox-tongue toes
feet blackened by sunshine, soled with bauxite and copper

feet that madden flies with their otherworldly musk
tapping the slow-slow beat of dirges on my church forecourts

feet that cart whimper-babies and dizzy-dads out of my drought lands
that yoke a plough when the oxen are exhausted and my soil too tough

bare feet of Wollo and Tigray and Gojjam that are long and thin and
    gloriously leathered
that have never been shod and are their own shoes! their own
    shoe-laces!

feet dribbling a sockball, planting the crack of a whip
wading into my great pelican lakes riddled with bilharzia and cow-piss

feet that tick out marathons on the wooded slopes of Arsi
or scamper down hill-tracks to escape the shufti of the Ogaden (or any
    brigand looking for boots with an AK-47)

feet tripping towards the delirious shade of thorn bushes regardless
    of the risk of hyena or porcupine

and feet that leave their little bones in me, like Lucy, earliest
    woman, light and pigeon-toed

feet that chatter about the past
                    feet that jump into the future

Poem to Friday

after a festive Oromo song

O Friday! be friendly
you rain on our tin roof
you wet-shoe my Pap
and hair-soak my Mam

O Friday! be friendly
it's end-of-week dinner
weekly fry-day for fish
weekly cuddle for Mam

O Friday! be friendly
tell the nile perch, be crispy
tell the peppers, be prickly
soak our bread in rich sauce

O Friday! be friendly
Mam's dropping her frypan
Pap's ouching and hopping
my brothers are scrapping

O Friday! be friendly
shrink the egg on Pap's big toe
throw salt on my brothers
jump our fish off the floor

O Friday! be friendly
don't dark while we're eating
don't water our feet –
keep our happiness dry!

Dirge for Mrs Ethiopia

*in the voices of at least ten boys aged eight to twelve, sometimes singing alone,
sometimes in twos or threes and sometimes all together*

Whose legs swell like a river?
whose ankles burst open like watermelons in the sun?

> *wai amlaki!*
> *wai-wai-wai!*

it is our Mother whose legs are ruined
our Mother, the always singing and laughing woman
her generous thighs slapped like a hundred drums
    when she pounded the t'ef
her smooth oily knees clicked like bicycle gears
    when she chased a chicken

> *wai amlaki!*
> *wai-wai-wai!*

we are the boys who visit, holding a daisy and an orange
we are the sick boys, too, on our clanky beds and trolleys
    malaria boys!
    bilharzia boys!
even the little red-boy shivering to himself in a corner

> *wai amlaki!*
> *wai-wai-wai!*

Mother! you were always laughing
even yesterday at five after the doctor's visit and the long
    injections and the cinnamon tea
you were humming like a Friday afternoon girl
you were smiling like a Sunday morning lady
so our Ward Sister clacked her tongue and said
araa! my auntie, why so giggle, when you are very sick?

wai amlaki!
wai-wai-wai!

look now! the sun is bright this morning
but our hearts are full of clouds
we are the dark boys beating our chests to clay
tying white cloths around our necks

wai amlaki!
wai-wai-wai!

wait, Mother! do not run off yet on your afterlife legs
look at us pouring out of our classrooms
and jumping out of our sickbeds
we will shake the sleepy churches and hunt the pitiless mosquito
we will clap and wail and question every teacher
   every politician!
   every nurse and clerk!

wai amlaki!
wai-wai-wai!

because we are struggling, Mother
who will carry us if you are lying down?
who will care for us if the box of your traditional and modern
   medicines rattles like a pea?
who will laugh for us
when we have lost our sense of humour?

wai amlaki!
wai-wai-wai!

wai amlaki: woe to God! (Amharic)
t'ef: fine grain used for making injera bread

Turkey of the Revolution

Bird who pounces on little grains
in case they run away
who swaggers his blood-red scarf, black eye-patch

    gruuk! gruuk!

now you march on the capital
ayee! a dust-devil blowing down the street
oyoo! a bomb shaking its own fuse

they have clipped your wings, turkey, is this what you cannot forgive?
you pull your farmer on a string, the shy one, skinny
his people are starving in Wollo, but he is not so angry as you

Christmas Eve, now Asfaw slits your throat
and boils you in a big clay pot
roasts you with eucalyptus leaves, red onions, cranberries

but, turkey! you still hang on to your toughness
you kick us with your stringy legs, shouting

    gruuk! gruuk!

even as our teeth come down and cut-cut

The banquet

after a photograph by Shimelis Desta, court photographer to Haile Selassie

Eyoha! Haile Selassie
King of Kings
and your shining guest, Elizabeth

it is night-time, maybe twelve
you burst through walls of flash photography
waving little finger wands

are you conjuring the spirits?
are you bewitching your peoples?

daytime beggars show us sores and stumps
stick hungry babies under our noses
even your lions have no teeth in the sunshine!

but at night, you throw the ugly out
put the young and restless in their beds
and switch on all the lights in your squares and palaces

then policemen bounce up on the stage and sing like whistles
imperial guards play saxophones in natty suits
and parents rush off with a little kiss to the Romanians!
    or *Hamlet* in Amharic!

then on to Zebra for a drink (or is it Dik-Dik?)
where the swizzle sticks are made of gold
and gunfights crackle like the gangsters in a poster
    at Ras Hailu's cinema

and somewhere in the shadows of the banquet
where tables groan with meat and fish
my mother is swishing her lovely ballgown

she has spent the afternoon backcombing her hair
    into a fairytale
stiffening it with puffs of Elnett
sliding her warm bosoms into the tipsy balcony

so she can dote on my father's arm, just out of sight
and he will still stand there stiffly, beaming

To the man with a guzzler wife

You who have a guzzler wife
divorce her and wait for me
                        famine poem from Northern Showa

My name is Dubbala, voice of famine
I am a hot wind in the marketplace
soon I will hammer on your flimsy door

here I am with wide-open eyes
with my eyes that are burning
you should look for a shrub to hide under!

I will suck the water from your rivers
chew the beans on your coffee bushes
brown the grass so your cows shrink to no-milk

do not boast you are so-and-so's friend
do not big-talk you are the son of Mr Rich
I have seen you by the road with your begging bag

the last injera is baked but brother swears to brother
    I have not one inch of eating left!
yes! salvation of the soul is a thing of the past

I am bad days coming and days that are worse than that
I am the end of *here comes a donkey loaded with lentils*
the start of *I swapped my mother for a taba of beans*

I am the green algae choking your well-water
the hand who gives your sister to the vultures
the poor are beating me, oh! the rich hurt my eyes

The epigraph is from one of the poems gathered in *Unheard Voices: Drought, Famine and God in Ethiopian Oral Poetry* by Fekade Azeze. My poem is a collage of lines freely adapted from Dr Azeze's book in homage to the amazing poems in that book.

Lizard waits for a new regime

Cool lick of zinc
with a long armoured tail
plated lizard! chief of the empty village
when soldiers come
we scream down every path
but you slip quietly under a rock

sly lizard! you can wait better than anyone
you have the patience of a dead person

when we creep back to our shadows
our buried pots
here you are like a bookmark
soaking up the sun, fixing us
with your unblinking UN observer eyes

do you scorn us for being so twitchy?
boast the fat cricket thrashing in your lips?

well-clothed lizard!
you are smart and resourceful
you do not beg or pray
even your tongue is on the lookout
and when it rains
you shine like a tank

weyra

wanzey

tid

& grar

shembeko

werka

hareg-

vine

& ficus

fool's

oak

sausage-

tree

*

how

could

a boy

not long

to cut

a zeng

or dulla

out of

words

like

these?

shenkora

cinnamo

WOLF-FENCES TUKUL-

ROADSIDE TABL

OW!!OW!!OW!!OW!!OW!!
(boy who stole the bread)

goattappingdonkeywhackingoxdrivingjerrycancartingpoopedarmpropping

aaaaaaa

nnnnnnn!!

RIBS   ROOF-BONES
-FOOTIE LEGS

bendy brass-topped prayer-stick
to lean on in church
when your throat's parched
and
the
priest
slowly
recites
the
miracle
of
Mary
and
the
Thirsty
Dog
when
She
took
off
her
shoe
and
wow!
it
was
full
of
water

Zerihun's granny calling, "have you swallowed a stick??" if he didn't bend to kiss her, laughing, "have you swallowed a stick??" if he wouldn't bend to her opinion

DONKEY-BACK FIREWOOD BUNDLES
OLD-WOMAN-BACK FIREWOOD BUNDLES

BOOM!   KOL

DRUMSTICK-WHO-CALLS-

OUTSIDE THE EMPERORS TENT,
BEFORE THE BATTLE WHICH WILL
COST HIM HIS LIFE, THEY PLANT
A FLAG-POLE, THE WIND FLUTTERS

long peaceful notes of bamboo flutes
long peaceful flute-fingers

TOOTHBRUSH TWIGS
& TINY NOBBLED GUMFLOSSERS

MY CHRISTMAS HOCKEY STICK! MY KOMET
FIRED AND OILED TO BASH IN YOUR TEMPLES

WITH
ITS
LARGE
SHINY
KNOB

OFA   BOOM!

OUR-COUNTRY-TO-WAR

my sister's smooth paddle for churning
is the colour of hard work and cream

nothing exists except this shekerkerit running and bouncing in front of a stick in front of a small boy

I am a bolt of canvas over two thick ash spars. Come, four men, lift my sick lady to the nearest clinic, fast as you can, five little miles over the warm mountains – it will be much quicker than calling an ambulance, even if there was one, which would have to tiptoe there and back on a tripwire of hairpin bends, loose rocks, bolshy goats

YOUNG SCRIBE BENDING HIS BEAUTIFUL LONG NECK OVER A CURVY REED PEN

UPRIGHTNESS.....SIMPLICITY.....DIGNITY

subsistence?   hardship?   hunger?

stick people

What have shepherds sung?

… the Emperor communicated with his regional viceroys:
'How has the country passed the night? What are people saying?
  What have shepherds sung?'
                    Aberra Jembere, *Agony in the Grand Palace*

They are the gentlest boys on earth
working rough hillsides
above the thorn-fenced farms and villages
already high enough to be forgotten

only a crook or bony shoulder breaks
the skyline
but each sheep bleats differently for them
they love the hundred tricky ways to sift and count

and when a shepherd starts to sing
he fills the valley
with three notes of longing
for the unseen life which he already leads

Small nervous prayer

By Salgawata'el
and Sabatna'el
by your name Iyu'el which crushed panthers of fire
by your secret names which are caves of refuge but may also be filled
  with toothy bats
by the names of the four terrifying beasts six-winged and seven-eyed
  who carry your throne the size of a golden building
by the names of the five nails driven through your hands and feet
  called *Sator Arepo Tenet Opera Rotas* which can be read both
  forwards and backwards on a crust of bread and dabbed three
  times on the wound from a rabid dog
by Berhana'el
and Afrataw
and Adna'el
save me from the demon who jumps out of the third graveyard
and eats the memories of children

Based on E.A. Wallis Budge's translation of the *Lefafa Tsedeq* (*Bandlet of Righteousness*), an early Ethiopic book of invocations of *asmat*, the secret names of Jesus with the power to ward off a variety of evils.

A cow in the sky

from an Amharic proverb: 'I have a cow in the sky, but I have not yet seen the milk'

There was once a boy in a white-painted house
  I have a cow in the sky!
  a cow in the sky!
who spilled some warm milk on the clean kitchen floor
  I have a cow in the sky!
  a cow in the sky!
the cook was annoyed to see that warm milk on the clean kitchen floor
of the white-painted house
  I have a cow in the sky!
  a cow in the sky!
but the boy laughed out loud to see the cook frown at the pool of
warm milk on the clean kitchen floor
  watat alleu! said the boy
   watat alleu!
and the angry cook smiled as the boy stuck his tongue in the pool of
warm milk on the clean kitchen floor of the white-painted house
  I have a cow in the sky!
  a cow in the sky!
  now I have tasted her milk!

watat alleu: there is milk (Amharic)

The shoes he does not have

'… our Empire was barefoot, skinny, with all its ribs showing.'
Ryszard Kapuschinski, *The Emperor*

Some people eye-pity his big bare feet

> *oyoo, blisters of Poverty!*
> *ayee, black soles of Despair!*

but he says

> *does a lion wear boots?*
> *does a goat go to the shoe shop?*

once he climbed a mountain
and prayed to St Gabriel of Kulubi
to unzigzag his big toe
then he wrote a long dusty poem about it
which was very kind to the saint
even though his toe remained completely bent

some boys point and sneer
some smart ladies on the corner panic and nose-peg

> *waiii! is this the pong of peasants who jump*
> > *down our rulers' throats?*
> *is this the fishiness of students who wisecrack about 30 million farmers*
> *and only 1 pct of our national budget spent on agriculture?*

but he just smiles his big bare teeth

> *ladies! the shoes I do not have*
> > *are not political*
> *they do not carry a gun or dream of throwing bricks*
> > *at a policeman*

then he goes off down the road singing

down with shoes!
down with socks!
down with poems about money!

Eucalyptus trees

Peering over the walls of boyhood, full face
to a long-armed wind

swinging their feathery teenage heads against the lemons
of a clear sky

these tall speckled jumpers
fast-growing firewood
in soils so light they can fly!

tremendous leapings over ripple-tin roofs
over the hundred-year fires they stoke
shedding endless strings of bark as if they were rich youths
   rewarding beggars

and when I shin up towards the first minty branch
it is too high!

so I make a fist with my knees and the trunk digs patterns in my skin
marks me with its smoky scent

as if the tree is hugging me back
as if it is saying goodbye

Boast of the fly-whisk

Tail without a horse! hair of the horse called
   Smoke-with-a-Tail
fierce flayer of wasps and fleas

I salute you, Gashay! relaxing on this cushy knee
   in sunny slug-warm garden

but here come
two fat scuttle flies
with feet
for stink and sick

Master! who wears his hang-dog like a shirt
do not throw me down and let the bandits suck your tongue

   life is meaningless, you wail,
    let them feast on me!

but I am your rope-handled warrior
from the bus to school
from the sweaty streets of Mercato where meat buzzed so loud
   it lived!

do not believe the mild voice of whisk
   (such a soft name!)
tell me, who thrashed the loutish hornet when you were six?
who shattered the pack of carrot flies?

would I whimper now, would I cringe, when you are ready to slide
   off your lion-skin chair?

Master! brandish me like a kalash
my grizzly mane is itching for a fight

gashay: respectful name for an older man, literally 'my shield' (Amharic)
kalash: short for Kalashnikov

Cupboards and a guitar

Most people die once, that is the general rule
death does not like people who die twice or more

  it is too much work!
   too much grief!

but Abebe, the slim good-looking boy, who became a man
when I was not looking
when I was out collecting firewood

the skilful carpenter whose cupboards have been called brave and
    devoted
because they defend their contents against all enemies

whose guitar playing was so clear and natural that it was compared
    to the sound of walking
this generous boy has just died for the third time!

first, in my head, during the Red Terror, his smiling body shot to
    pieces at a demo
or thrown at Eritrea like a hand grenade
MiG-deafened, squandered, exploded in a gully, left to wither in his
    green fatigues
the wind not even knowing he was dead

then again, five years ago, from dragon beer and t'ej, slumped on a
    carpet of empties
in his crumpled dirty shirt, alone a week before they found him
and his lips that had lost their grin

  eyuu! loose wire of a batchelor

who fathered cupboards and songs, while all around, his sturdy
    friends were busy
making eight or ten God-fearing boys and girls
to populate the country with good milky smells and talking

and now today, a Monday, off the Yeka Road where he lived as a boy
Abebe dies for the third time
when Aster's son says

    Abebe died of drink
    yes! Abebe died

and you, his mother and sisters and cousins
you, his many customers and admirers
look! how he continues to die when our thoughts fly to him like
  songbirds

when we gather to praise him
and listen to his guitar
with every ear in our head and our hearts
and a thin scratchy voice that is so modest we had almost forgotten it

    a voice that slips out of our ears!

is singing Abebe's version of Bob Dylan or Tilahoun
or when we spot a cupboard in a shop window whose sturdy doors
  shout

    nothing inside us will come to any harm!

because if Abebe was the kind of boy whom death loves like a brother
who dies just once
that his dust settles lightly and quick

how could he keep on tumbling off the shelf of our mind's eye
and break into a hundred songs?

Red Terror: the campaign of murder unleashed by Col. Mengistu's regime in 1977
t'ej: strong honey wine, like mead with a mule kick
Tilahoun Gessesse: the biggest star of Ethiopian music, known as 'the Voice', died
  in 2009

The dugout copy of Jerusalem

After a swarm attacked the prince's cot
but did not sting, his mother cried and called him
Lalibela: *the bees recognise his sovereignty!*
and when he became king, he had a dream
to make a new Jerusalem
not building upward in the normal way
but take this close-to-heaven mountaintop
far from lowlanders and prying eyes
and ask his masons to dig down, as if to say

we will hear the word of God more clearly
if we mine the silence of the earth!

So, helped by angels with strong hands
stonecutters from Egypt, India
even Templars, some men say
the rocks and soil were levered out, pit-edges scooped
facades and wood-beam windows mimicked out of stone
cross-naves and tabot-chambers hollowed
smoothed and painted, dressed with incense, silks
as if they had been waiting since the birth of time
to be not built, but just unearthed, discovered!

Now his eleven blood-red churches stood
below the surface of the mountaintop
and dawn seeped through their doorways like a cat,
deacons beat their muffled drums
as the sun picked out a single tree to mark the Mount of Olives,
while that curiously uplifting smell of early morning bread
wafted, sleepy pilgrim, from the bethlehem of Mary's House
and priests hummed words that no one really understood
except a few old monks who were deaf or just not listening…

then Lalibela, king of men who still after a thousand years
are cutting churches out of tufa cliffs
still burrowing in gloom and prayer for what it means
to be a builder of something that is fragile and remote, even from
   itself,
but as important to our world and wellbeing as bees…
and while a novice in his musty orange robe crouched on a step
droning passages from Enoch's book
King Lalibela threaded his sandals, took his two sons
by the hand and walked downhill from the wonders.

bethlehem: house of bread (Hebrew)

Gifts

Her waterfalls white-pouring
out of fig roots
over the slippery feet of boulders
and baboons
on golden hilltops
her spate of luscious
blue-green baubles
cascading through clefts
and chasms
taking the soft butter of the sun
to Egypt and Sudan
throwing her shy waters of vegetation
up to the deltas
her blessings against dust
and poverty

goodbye my liquid jewels!

her old encrusted roasting pan, one-woman-band of taps and popping
in a house of little boys who wake up every morning to the dream
of Ennat's coffee… her special mix, her hum and clicks, quick pinch
  of rue
and that a larky goat lives out there in the yard, who first went silly
munching beans which now we pick and sack and sell, containerise
and ship around the world, un-dock, de-stuff, weigh up and brew

my hello tastings of Harar, Langani, Sidamo!

attics of silence
mountains
glowing like skin
a talking so languid it has to lie down
her stubbled lake-islands, no women, no hens
radiant salesgirls who whisper like stones
her hermits, her cranks
her poets, her monks

... and who else would house them?
whose giddy, whose roomy, whose crumb?

Zenabu's taxi

Quick! let's jump into Zenabu's small chapel of dryness
    on this big-rains afternoon
let's slide our bottoms up the pew
and sit here gratefully as prayer-books
while Addis Ababa goes floating past the window like a fish…

Zenabu, whose soft watery name means *it's raining!*

whose neck is glistening a rosary of sweat
    under the hairline
this priestly Man United fan
born the day God said: *enough's enough!*
and broke the drought with one huge leather ball of rain…

Zenabu sees it washing over him, that mighty water and the blood!

so now he hangs a Virgin Mary from his crackled
    rearview mirror
gums a Rooney poster-icon on the door
and when he jams a tape in the rusty deck
it's got to be his treasured two-cassette collection –
the All-Time Greatest Hits of Kidus Uriel's Boy-Deacons' Choir…

kidus: saint (Amharic)

Before a meal

Take the water and the soap
take the shiny water kettle and the dish of grainy soap
lift the shiny water kettle's lengthy spout
and when his hands have touched the dish
when his hands have swallowed up the grainy soap
then pour! pour! pour!
then say: *is it enough?*
and when he says: *some more!*
then pour again until his hands are soft and brown
until his fingers glisten and his palms are pink
and cleanness flows up his arms and face
and lights his eyes as he eats

Two brothers

Two times nine or ten
two tufts of hair by a bus-stop on Bole Road

you are not bark and tree
you are not lunatics chained together

one of you has all the grinning
one of you has a pale blot on his forehead as if his thoughts
    are burning a way out
one of you always wins at the whip game

some day you will separate
and the earth will shake her head because she knows

two brothers are tough as a coffee pan
two brothers have four feet quick as a kob escaping the leopard
    and twenty fingers for unpicking tricky knots
two brothers can get through

  how logical is my brother!
  how colourful is my brother!

two arms hanging round each other's shoulder
two arms swinging on their own

two tufts of hair: the so-called *kuncho* cut, common for boys in Ethiopia, particu-
larly small ones. All the hair is shaved except for a small round or oval mohawk at
the centre-front, which is said to be useful for angels to pull a boy out of trouble!

About the fish in Lake Langano

I have pitched my tent, Abebe, by the lake
night-long in lake breezes
where pebbles crackle cooling
and a thorn acacia scratches at the sky

I wait for you to appear after the years
and take me fishing
somewhere tonight you are sitting again
on the sand of my thoughts
untying your shoes

all around is the rustle of sleeping flamingos
crunch of turtles
and way off in the bush
a shuffle that could be hunting dogs
or a cowherd turning over

do the fish know we're coming, Abebe?
our whispers inch into the silt
our hooks quiver like mosquitoes, prick the water

and as you bend again
into a jaunty boy
hoick your trousers to the knee
I can hear the catfish rise up bubbling

it is too long since he came
it is too long since he bent forward
and called us to him...

this need in the heart of all beings to be fished

The goodbye tree

A tree on the Shola road
   wanzey! wanzey!
old priest with his parasol of leaves
   shady! shady!
summoning cool green breezes
   heavenly! heavenly!
donkeys scratch their backs on him, dogs piss on his foot
   ugly! ugly!
a father who embraces his son and a mother who weeps
   openly! openly!
this is how it is to be almost a man
   jittery! jittery!
with a suitcase by the road-side, with a bus throwing all personal
  things up on the roof
   risky! risky!
a boy who is leaving, his road descends the mountain like a careless
  goat
   scary! scary!
his life is a distant day that was only this morning, even his bag of
  roasted corn tastes different now
   chalky! chalky!
but what about new friends in the city? what about becoming a
  dandy in uncle's car-repair shop?
   proudly! proudly!
a tree behind him on the Shola road
   wanzey! wanzey!
a tree standing tall and quiet like a prayer
   whispery! whispery!
a tree that waves him away on the big road
   goodbye! goodbye!

wanzey: *Cordia africana*, a large tree used for shade on roads and coffee plantations,
  for log hives, beer barrels and furniture; its leaves are used to treat wounds and
  skin diseases

MISE EN PAGES ET TYPOGRAPHIE :
LES ÉDITIONS DU BORÉAL

ACHEVÉ D'IMPRIMER EN FÉVRIER 2001
SUR LES PRESSES DE L'IMPRIMERIE AGMV MARQUIS
À CAP-SAINT-IGNACE (QUÉBEC).